Daily Devotional Prescriptions for the Soul

DEDICATION

In Joyful Service

Dedicated to all the Nurse Practitioners who share the love of Jesus during a day of caring for God's children. His blessings bring opportunities to comfort others in times of need. Other times a cheerful heart is required. The friendship Jesus gives us inspires us to keep going at all times.

ACKNOWLEDGMENTS

Thanks to all who shared a piece of their heart in each devotion and
Bible verse. God's word is our inspiration. It is the hope of the editors
that prayerful reading of this devotional book brings special
encouragement to walk on God's path with an attitude of Joyful
service.
Cover photo was taken by Ruth Chong, MSN, FNP-C
at Ala Moana Beach in Oahu, Hawaii
Cover design by Miki Wright, Lexington, KY

Day 1

Jesus said, "Ask and you will receive. Seek and you will find. Knock and the door will be opened to you." (Matthew 7:7)

One of the most significant realizations we, as Christians, can come to is that we cannot do all God would want us to do without his help. We cannot accomplish what we would want to accomplish and know we ought to do by our own strength alone. We need to ask for strength and guidance from God. We need to pause periodically and seek help through prayer. When we encounter a situation in life we don't know how to handle, we need only to knock and the door will be opened for us.

Prayer enables us to do what we are unable to do by our own strength. O God, grant that, through prayer, our capacities for service to you may be greater and our channels of your abundant resources of love may come into our hearts and life. Amen.

In loving memory of the life and ministry of Dr. M. Glynn Burke
By Dr. Rosemary Elizabeth Burke Minnick, DNP, APRN, FNP-C
Adjunct Faculty Indiana Wesleyan University Graduate School of Nursing, Visiting Professor Chamberlain College of Nursing

Day 2

A friendly smile makes you happy, and good news makes you feel
strong.
Proverbs 15:30   Contemporary English Version (CEV)
FACE LIFT
Conference meetings are both delightful and draining. Everyone
gathered with hopes of hearing new ideas about how to share the joy of
Jesus in their health outreach. Community members were suffering
from unimaginable struggles. Tense moments were lifted up in prayer.
Then a photographer came to take pictures of the board. Smiles were
scare. The photographer said "Peace filled the room after the prayer."
Everyone looked up in surprise. "And I heard joyful chatter as people
walked out of the meeting. Sharing Jesus' love made them strong. "
The board stood up straight and shouted "Thanks be to God!" Now
they felt strong. Each member looked at the photographer who had a
twinkle in her eye and friendly smile. Click. "I now have a picture of a
happy group! All you needed was a facelift- good news and a smile will
do that!"
Dear God, as I am aware of struggles in my community, let me also be
aware of the peace around me. May the good news of Jesus love make
me feel strong. May I have a smile that makes others happy. And may
I know that this is your will. Amen

Dr. Joan Graham Nathan, D.N.P- Nurse Practitioner in private
internal medicine office on Long Island, New York; Parish Nurse,
retired Nursing professor at Suffolk Community College, Stony Brook
University Nursing Alumni Board member, COFNP Trustee and
author of devotionals written to joyfully share God's word.

Day 3

And he said to them "It is not for you to know times or seasons which the Father has put in His own authority." (Acts 1:7)

God's timing is something that most of us struggle with from time to time. In a society of instant gratification we want it now, not tomorrow, next week, or next year, but right now.

As a young married couple my husband and I desperately wanted to start a family. As the years went by and we did not conceive we became sad and discouraged. Through heartache God led us to adoption. As I began digging into the idea of adoption I found and agency named "Bless This Child." It was in this moment that I felt a peace that I had been struggling to find. After a phone call to the adoption agency I knew God had worked it all out according to his plan, not ours. After 9 months we welcomed home a perfect Russian princess. As if the adoption was not enough affirmation that God was fulfilling his plan in our lives, we were pregnant five months after our adoption. Although God's timing is difficult to accept at times, when reflecting, the pure awesomeness of his wisdom is evident.

Dear Heavenly Father thank you for your perfect timing, you are the master of perfection and for that we are forever grateful.

In honor of my husband Jonathan and our children Sidney, Sami, and Cash
By Ashlei Jobe, APRN, NP-C
Idabel Primary Care and May's Hospice

Day 4

"My sheep listen to my voice; I know them, and they follow me."
John 10:27, NLT
Learning to follow Jesus has taken practice. It didn't come naturally
because early in my adult walk I really didn't understand what it meant
to be led by Jesus. One day our pastor suggested we follow his practice
of rising in the morning and spend time in God's word and listen for
Holy Spirit to tell us what He was saying.
Years later, spending time in God's word in the morning is a habit for
me with my first cup of coffee. I enjoy listening and learning from
Him. Scripture jumps out that is relevant to my situation at that time.
Holy Spirit's lessons have changed and shaped me and guided me. I
have grown to a prophetic artist and do stage painting for my church.
This was not natural for me. It is through his grace I have learned to
paint to glorify Him. This piece of art is a prophetic piece I did,
inspired by scripture.

Father, thank you for showing me that you are speaking to me every
day through your word, as well as the world around me. Your words
are a comfort. Thank you for the peace of your consistent guidance.

In honor of my church family and the leaders of Dayton Vineyard,
Dayton, Ohio, who continually teach and strengthen the walk of our
members. Thank you Doug and Marcy Roe and all of the pastors who
lead us.
Cheryl Dunlap, APRN,

Day 5

"Since you put away lying, speak the truth, each one to his neighbor, because we are members of one another. Be angry and do not sin. Don't let the sun go down on your anger, and don't give the Devil an opportunity." Ephesians 4: 25-27.

As God's children, we must remember to treat each other with honesty, respect and love, even during conflict. It may not always be easy to be friends with everyone, but the Bible reminds us not to allow ourselves lose control of our emotions and sin out of anger. Satan gets great pleasure watching us fight each other. Our God was strong enough to part the seas; he surely can help us control our emotions.

Dear Lord,
Thank you for giving us the opportunity to help you heal others. Please help us to be honest, respectful and love our brothers and sisters. Help us to remember to control our emotions and forgive others when times are tough. It is only through your strength that we can fight Satan and his desire for conflict. We love you and are so grateful for the life that you have blessed us with. Amen.

Melissa Bell, MSN, APRN, FNP-C
Rapid Response CPR, LLC- owner
Urgent Care- Nurse Practitioner
Post Acute Care & Skilled Nursing- Nurse Practitioner
Washington, DC

Day 6

They are reborn-not with a physical birth resulting from human passion or plan, but a birth that comes from God. (John 1:13 NLT)

It was my moment to say goodbye and thank my patient for allowing me to be a part of her life at such a vulnerable moment in time. She pulled me in closer and our eyes locked as if to tell me heaven was a destination not a place, and she would soon be there. I fought back tears as she thanked me for comforting and caring for her. Then by some miracle, a hospital room was transformed into the labor room of heaven and she passed away peacefully surrounded by those she loved. Like a midwife, I was privileged to be present while another soul was delivered home.

Remind us Lord that death is not the end. May we always remember that we have the honor of being called to minister to those who are preparing to enter into your presence.

In loving memory of my parents, Sara and Luis Villegas and my mother-in-law, Charmaine Prendergast, whose delivery home came too soon. By Elena Prendergast, DNP, APRN, FNP-C, Palliative Care Nurse Practitioner and owner of Tree of Life Health Consultant, LLC.

Day 7

Galatians 6:4 = "Each one should test their own actions. Then they can take pride in themselves alone, without comparing themselves to somebody else."

It never fails to happen. I'm content. I'm happy with myself. Life is good! Then BAM - I start to compare my house, my kids, my looks, etc. with those around me.

What happened that changes my outlook so suddenly? I truly believe it's because I take my eyes off being thankful for what I have and I focus on what I lack.

When I focus on all God's blessed me with (a husband who loves me, multiple vehicles so I can go where I want when I want, the opportunity to further my education, the privilege of home schooling my 4 children, and on and on) I won't see my lack but my wealth!

Father, help us to focus on your gifts to us and not what we feel You are withholding. Thank you for all the blessings You've showered on us. You are a good Father who loves to lavish His children with good gifts!

By Jen Larson, RN, BSN

MSN/FNP student at Cedarville University in Cedarville, Ohio

Day 8

I was in a point in my nursing career, where I was feeling burned out. I was physically & mentally drained. I was questioning my role as a nurse, thinking I needed a change. I wanted something other than caring for others. I had been working in Intensive Care Unit for many years, & I was ready to quit. Then, I connected with a family of an elderly Native American Woman who was my patient. She'd had a major stoke & was on life support. After a week in the ICU, family decided it was time to withdraw life support. I was lucky to be assigned to the patient that day. She died "beautifully" with family at bedside. Emotional, I went home feeling a loss, but also a deep sense of rebirth. I posted the following on Facebook that evening. In ways I cannot explain, this experience saved my nursing career:

A Small Reflection of Our Role as ICU Nurses.

As nurses, we want to heal, and save lives. Sometimes it's not just about saving lives. It's about saying a healing prayer with a family while holding their dying loved one's hand. It's about singing a beautiful hymn and feel spirituality fill the room. It's hearing a family give permission to their loved one to let go, and being witness to their breaking hearts as the patient seems to hear them and fade away. It's hearing them ask the Lord to take accept their loved one and take her home, and literally FEEL a presence in the room. It's the peacefulness and beauty as they pray, sing, and almost rejoice, after telling them their loved one is gone.

It's acceptance into their sacred family circle as they include you & make you feel like you are part of their family. Then, it's the gifts they give you in return for the work you have done.

Those gifts are the countless hugs, the many "thank you's," and the "I won't forget you's." Those are the gifts we take home with us, and they are invaluable.

You then realize... Maybe it really is about HEALING.

Healing from the stress and fatigue that comes with this job. Healing from the "why do I stay in this profession?" Healing from the many challenges of this role. You then realize the purpose of your day. And you realize just how privileged you really are to have the opportunity to be part of this experience. And all that negativity seems to dissipate & you are ready for the next one.

Conrad Cordova, MSN APRN FNP-C.
Family Nurse Practitioner & currently manage patients in Skilled Nursing Facilities.

Day 9

For the Glory of God

For me, the hardest part of being a believer is living the Christian life. By that I mean that I find it difficult to do *everything* for the Glory of God. How do I glorify God when I've just admitted the same patient I've seen for the fifteenth time... this month? By welcoming him as Christ has welcomed me, for the glory of God (Rom. 15:7).

You see, I'm as human as the next person. I (we) must understand that our faith, our salvation, isn't supposed about health, wealth, prosperity, fame, security, or anything else. Our salvation is supposed to be about living our lives in such a way "that in everything God may be glorified through Jesus Christ" (1 Pet. 4:11). What better place for us to do that than in our clinical practices! Welcome them as Christ welcomed us. Often, you don't have to say anything about faith or salvation because they will ask... just like my patient did. He left, feeling better... about life, and with a restored faith. He was reminded of his profession of faith many years ago.

"For FROM him and THROUGH him and TO him are all things. To HIM be glory forever. Amen." Romans 11:36
Father, show me how to do everything in life for your glory... even when I don't want to.

Mark Davis, FNP-C
Husband, Dad, Servant of Christ

Day 10

Yet you, LORD, are our Father. We are the clay, you are the potter; we are all the work of your hand. (Isaiah 64:8)

While at a yard sale one day, I noticed a crockpot. It was in good shape on the outside, but dirty, and stained on the inside and was going to be thrown away if no one took it. I took the crockpot home, and filled it with hot, soapy bleach water. After a while, I poured out the dirty water and all the stains were gone! I then placed a roast inside and a short time later, dinner was done. Despite the dirty stains, it did exactly what it was created to do. I was reminded that we are like this crockpot, stained and dirty with sin. But just like the hot soapy water removed the stains from the crockpot, the Blood of Jesus can cleanse us of our sins so we can do the job He created us to do.

Lord, forgive me of my sins and wash me whiter than snow. Help me fulfill your will for my life so I can be all you created me to be. Amen.

By Sharon Laubenstein, ARNP, FNP-BC
Nurse Practitioner for Integrated Care Professional providing care to geriatric patients.

"Therefore if any man be in Christ, he is a new creature: old things are passed away; behold, all things are become new." --II Corinthians 5:17

In a little shop in Kailua, Hawaii, I purchased a beautiful green and white glass turtle that had been crafted from fragments of sea glass. I've thought about the beautiful creations designed from glass objects that have been tossed into the ocean. The waves crash the glass against the rocks and reefs, shattering the glass until it finds its way to the sandy shore, where it is picked up by an artist, who turns the broken pieces into a masterpiece.

God finds us wherever we are and picks up the broken fragments of our lives and shapes each of us into a "new creation."

Heavenly Father, help us to remember that Your redeeming grace is for everyone. Amen.

By Ruth Chong, APRN, FNP-C
Jackson, Mississippi

Day 12

"And the Lord, He is the One who goes before you. He will be with you, He will not leave you nor forsake you; do not fear nor be dismayed (Deuteronomy 31:8)."

Often times life can become overwhelming and we can lose sight of goals and aspirations when fear and doubt creeps in. Fear can be paralyzing and can hinder you from reaching your full potential in your personal life, as wives, husbands and as employees. Life has shown us that in many ways it can be unpredictable as we watch the daily news and this unpredictability has created a culture of fear in our society. We are constantly faced with death, disease, and violence that enhance those fears. However, as Christians, we have a perfect hope that if we put our trust in Him He will cast out the spirit of fear and replace it with His perfect peace. It is His promise that He will direct our paths and be our guide. This requires a mustard seed of faith on our part and a daily devotion to pray asking for strength and guidance.

Dear Father, we pray that you will be our constant guide and lead us on our daily walk. We pray that even in a world of unpredictability you cast all fears and replace with your perfect peace. Amen.

In loving memory of the life and ministry of my grandmother Leatha T. Jenkins

By Yolanda R. Greene, MSN, FNP-C

Day 13

Carry each other's burdens, and in this way you will fulfill the law of Christ. (Galatians 6:2)

As we pass through our days on this Earth we must be thankful for each blessing the Lord has given us. As many of us are blessed beyond measure we must understand that our call is to help one another. Be a blessing to others. Help those in need; allow the love of Christ to flow freely through you. Nursing is a blessed career that allows us to help lift others up each day, to be a difference maker for those we come in contact with daily. However we all need to do the same in our private lives. We need to be an example for those who come after us. Be someone's hero today and you will be a hero in God's eyes tomorrow.

Heavenly Father, May the love that you have for us flow through us to those we encounter. May we be an example of your love for others to witness through us, your greatness. Amen.

By Scotty Combs, APRN, MSN, NP-C
    Family Nurse Practitioner
    Juniper Health Inc.

Day 14

Peace in the Storm

John 16: 33 "I have told you these things, so that in me you may have peace. In this world you will have trouble. But take heart! I have overcome the world."

Difficult times should not come as a surprise to us because Jesus forecasted that we would have trouble in this world. In other words, He's telling us that there's 100% chance of rain, and unlike human weather forecasters, He is always right. But, we can take comfort in knowing that long before we hear the distant roll of thunder, see the first flash of

lightning or feel the first drop of rain on our face, God knows that the storm is coming, and He says to us "It's going to be okay. I have overcome the world!!"

Prayer: Lord, I praise you for the amazing, all-powerful, all knowing God that you are. Thank you for being with me always and giving me your peace, especially during the storms of life. Help me to live in you and through you so that my life will bring glory to you even when it rains.

Amen!

In loving memory of my amazing Mother, Anna Lou Mitchell Bennett

By Cynthia McMaken, MSN, APRN, FNP-C

Family Nurse Practitioner Five Rivers Health Center

Day 15

Ecclesiastes 3:1 states, "To everything there is a season, and a time to every purpose under the heaven."

We as Christians do not have control over events in our lives. Both time and season are controlled by the Lord. Chance meetings and bizarre circumstances are not coincidental. They are divine events designed to create a closer relationship between the believer and God. He directs our paths and guides our futures by his loving hands. He is in total control of all events that we encounter. We are powerless in determining our outcomes. When we acknowledge our limitations as men and women we become more open to the Lord's divine presence and power. In the presence of difficult seasons we are not left without a lifeline.

Prayer is the vessel used to connect with God to express our needs. When we engage in prayer we are drawn near to God and are open to hear His voice and instruction. Dear heavenly Father please bless us as we endure the seasons of life. Cover us and keep us in your protective arms. Amen.

Michelle K. Scott, MSN, ARNP, FNP-BC,
Graduate of Jacksonville University SON
Experienced in Acute, Post-Acute and Primary Care

Day 16

"For I know the plans I have for you," declares the Lord, "plans to prosper you and not to harm you, plans to give you hope and a future." (Jeremiah 29:11)

As imperfect humans living in an imperfect world, we all face hardship and pain but it is how we handle these things that helps to shape us into who we are. Do we let our pain become our destiny or do we give it to God? God sent his son Jesus Christ to die on the cross so that our sins, shame, and pain can be taken away and so that we can have eternal life with him in a beautiful Kingdom where there is no pain or sadness. We should openly accept this gift and not allow pain to be our destiny. God takes care of the birds, so how much more would he take care of you? God takes care of the flowers, so how much more will he take care of you? Scripture says we are not promised a perfect world here on earth but we are promised everlasting life in a perfect Kingdom when we accept Jesus as our Lord and Savior. Once we truly know Jesus, we know that his plans for us are far better than we could ever imagine. Will there be trials and pain? Sure, but Jesus already paid the price for us and we do not have to handle pain on our own. God wants us to be happy and with prayer and petition we need to give our requests to him and ask for God's will to be done in all situations. It may not always be what we want but he will give us what we need. God never gives us more than we can handle, even in our most difficult times. We just need to have faith in knowing that his plans for us are good and know that he is God and he can move mountains.

Dear Heavenly Father, please give us comfort and peace, especially, in those times when we feel like we don't know where to turn. When we feel weighed down by life's hardships, remind us that you sent your son Jesus to die on the cross so that we could be free from those chains that bind us. Please remind us that your plans for us are much better than we could imagine. Please help us to trust that despite what we may be going through that you alone can give us a hope and a future. May we love you and worship you not only in the good times but also the bad and always give you all of the glory. Amen.

In loving memory of Emma Marie Graziano, Mary Graziano, Regina Dombrowski, and Frank DeSanto. May you fly high with the angels.
By Melissa Osborne, MSN, ARNP, FNP-C Graduate of Georgetown University

Day 17

Isaiah 40:31 King James Version (KJV)

[31] But they that wait upon the LORD shall renew their strength; they shall mount up with wings as eagles; they shall run, and not be weary; and they shall walk, and not faint.

This verse became important after my daughter passed away from a chronic illness at age 18. I had never let the message it brings sink in. My daughter was physically week and had been in a wheelchair for about 10 years. When they read this verse at her funeral, it really came to mean a great deal. Over the past several years we had watched her become weaker and her health deteriorate. She was a very faithful Christian and didn't mind sharing her faith. She, as well as family and friends knew that after her passing she would be with Jesus in Heaven. This verse gave me reassurance that not only is she in Heaven, but her strength was renewed, and she did not walk, but ran to Jesus. With faith in our Lord, Jesus Christ, our faith and strength can be renewed. Have faith and believe in He who can do everything.

Dear Lord, please help us to renew our strength and our faith every day. Please allow us to use this renewal of strength and faith for the benefit of your kingdom. Bring us through trials and allow us to use this knowledge to help others in our daily work. Amen.

In loving memory of the life Susan Whitney Wright, loving daughter, granddaughter, and sister.

By Dr. Dawn R. Carpenter, DNP, APRN, FNP-C
Assistant Professor of Nursing, University of the Cumberlands
Nurse Practitioner, First Care Clinics

Day 18

Healing by faith

He is called the Great Physician because he heals all. We can spend a lifetime in actual time and money, looking to cure our diseases yet never coming to an actual cure that permanently changes our lives. The woman with the blood issue did exactly that. For twelve long years, she went from doctor to doctor, spending inconceivable amounts of money on any conceivable cure out there, but came up empty-handed and even grew worse. She became desperate and broken. During her time of desperation is when she heard about Jesus. Something happened to her when she heard about Jesus. She started believing that He could and would heal her to the extent that she said "If only I may touch his clothes, I shall be made well" (Mark5: 27) Acting on her belief, she made her way to Jesus and touched his Garment. Immediately, her bleeding stopped and she felt in her body that she was healed that very instant. Jesus, her true physician, also pronounced her healed by saying "Daughter, your faith has made you well" (Mark 5:34)

God is always ready and waiting to heal us from any and all our infirmities, no matter how impossible they seem to us. We should never allow the spirit of fear to keep us from approaching him. Once we approach him, be persistent, courageous, and desperate and unwavering in your faith, because it is only by faith that releases God's healing power.

Heavenly Father, today I come to you in faith, praying for healing over my sick body. Cover me, anoint me and let the blood that you shed on Calvary's cross flow through every vein, artery, and cell in my body. Restore me Lord Jesus and make me whole again. I receive the healing you have for me today in Jesus name, Amen.

By Elly Armah, FNP-BC, Clinic Manager Little Clinic, Arlington TN. Breast Cancer stage 3b survivor.

Day 19

Many things cause us to be afraid. Illness, finances, and relationships can all cause us to become anxious, even paralyzing us. God has a plan for us, even when we cannot see a path. He had a plan for the Israelites, and He has a plan for all of us, moving us forward to accomplish His will.

"And the LORD said to Moses, "Why do you cry to Me? Tell the children of Israel to go forward."
Exodus 14:15 NKJV

These words were said to Moses in a time of fear and uncertainty. We can face our fears when we know that He goes before us, beside us, and behind us.

Heavenly Father, We thank you giving us strength and for relieving our fears with your Word, Your presence, and faith to know that You are near. In Jesus Holy Name, Amen.

Cynthia M. Bratcher, MSN, APRN, FNP-C, CEN
Envision Physician Services
Emergency Medicine Lead Advanced Practice Provider
Bowling Green, KY

"Come to me, all you who are weary and burdened, and I will give you rest. Take my yoke upon you and learn from me, for I am gentle and humble in heart, and you will find rest for your souls. For my yoke is easy and my burden is light." (Matthew 11:28-30 **NIV**)

As nurse practitioners, the majority of our day is filled with duties and responsibilities associated with the provision of physical, mental, emotional, and spiritual health care for patients and families. Before and after clinic/hospital shifts, we are fulfilling our roles as wives/husbands, parents, brothers/sisters, grandparents, aunts/uncles, nieces/nephews, godparents, and friends. The nurse practitioner profession requires that we be lifelong learners and teachers; therefore, many of us are fulfilling the assignments of being graduate students and nurse educators. We often continue to meet our professional obligations even in the midst of our own personal trials and tribulations.

With all of these demands, nurse practitioners often neglect to properly care for themselves. We must remember to restore our own energy reserves after imparting the gifts of compassion, wisdom, understanding, counsel, fortitude, and knowledge to our patients and their families. Nurse practitioners can do this by spiritually communing and reconnecting with God on a daily basis for He is our primary source of strength and place of refuge.

Father God, please embody us with the physical, mental, emotional, and spiritual fortitude to provide health care to your people. Even when we become weary in performing our roles and responsibilities as nurse practitioners, you will remind us of the ethical oath we took and spiritual call we answered to serve individuals and families in our local, national, and global communities. In Jesus' Name, Amen.

By Antiqua Nicole Smart, DNP, APRN, FNP-BC, PHNA-BC

Board Certified Family Nurse Practitioner, Board Certified Advanced Public Health Nurse, Nurse Practitioner Visiting Professor

Psalm 91: 1-5
This I declare, that He alone is my refuge, my place of safety. He is my God, and I trust Him

The spring storm hurled ice pellets from the leaden sky. I looked out the window to see a mama dove sitting on the nest, her feathered back taking the brunt of the storm. I knew there were baby doves in the nest -only a few days old and completely vulnerable to the storm that raged around them. Their only protection was the Mama Bird that buffered the winds and ice, and whose soft feathers kept them warm and dry in the nest. As I watched the dove weather the storm over the next hours, I noticed that she held firm, never once leaving her babies, keeping them safe under her wings until the storm passed.

Isn't this how our Heavenly Father shelters us during those times when the winds of pain and fear threaten to blow us over? When the stresses and anxieties of life feel as sharp as ice pellets against our skin? He gathers us safe under His protection with the promise of His strength and faithfulness. We need only to whisper the name of Jesus and He is there, fighting for us, placing His mighty power between us and that which would do us harm.

Heavenly Father-

While the storms of life rage around me, I rest peacefully in your loving arms, knowing that you are stronger than any fear, any anxiety, any situation. Amen.

Tammy Degenhardt MSN, APNP, FNP-BC
Nurse Practitioner, CVS Minute Clinic
I have been blessed to be an RN for 30 years, witnessing the joy of the first breath, supporting those taking their last-and serving those suffering in between with the talents God has given me.

Day 22

His Work In Us

For I am confident of this very thing, that He who began a good work in you will perfect it until the day of Christ Jesus (Philippians 1:6).

As we walk through life and especially as we aspire to be near to God, we often realize that we fall short of our goal. Scripture tells us to be like Him. But we see Jesus in scripture and we know we are not like Him. Scripture tells us "You shall be Holy, for I am Holy" (1Peter 1:16). As we look at this verse in Philippians 1:6, we find a wonderful gift. It is God, through His Holy Spirit, who works in and through us to bring us into the likeness of Jesus. Sometimes that work brings us through joys, sometimes through sorrows. So in whatever you are experiencing today, lift it up to Jesus. Ask the Father to continue His work in you, leading and guiding you in the way to that perfect salvation.

Father God, in our weakness, we often walk away from you and become enamored with things of this world. Thank you for loving us through the cross of Christ and reaching down through the Holy Spirit to work in us your gift of salvation. Create in me a clean heart, acceptable to you in that day. Amen.

Dr. Teresa D. Schenck, DNP, ARNP, CPNP
Pediatric Nurse Practitioner,
Keokuk Community Health Center SE Iowa
Associate of Biblical Studies, Moody Bible Inst. Chicago

Day 23

Hebrews 13:2 Do not neglect to show hospitality to strangers, for thereby some have entertained angels unawares.

What a beautiful thought! In all of our daily hustle and bustle as health care healers, think about what it would mean to meet an angel disguised as a patient. Have you had the experience where an unexpected connection is made as you look in the eyes of a stranger who comes to you for help and healing? Perhaps this is a meeting with an angel messenger, and a time to pay attention to the message they bring us.

Hospitality has been defined as the generous, warm and friendly reception to others. Are you being hospitable to your angel? Do you need God's peace and calm to reach out to your angel?

Take a breath, center yourself in peace, and treat each person you encounter as one of God's angels. Be hospitable and listen with your heart for the angel's message to you.

O God, in the hustle and bustle of everyday life, help me to slow down, to welcome the angel messenger you send. Help me to see you in the eyes of each person I touch today.

In honor of those who serve others by their hands, their heads and their hearts.

By Dr. Marjorie Vogt, PhD, DNP, CNP

Faculty Ohio University School of Nursing

Day 24

Job 29:12 Because I rescued the poor who cried for help, and the fatherless who had none to assist them.

Being a survivor of child homelessness, abuse and neglect, I am so blessed to have been given the ability to pursue an education without family support or role models. God has been beside me, the best of Fathers, allowing me to impact the lives of others in providing compassionate nursing care while establishing a stable future for myself.

Father, guide my hands as I care for your people. Allow them to feel your love through my presence. Fill me with compassion, and give me courage to care for those most in need. Make me worthy, O Lord, for the tasks you have prepared for me today. Amen.

Christina Hartshorn, BSN. Family Nurse Practitioner student, expected graduation February, 2019.

Day 25

Matthew 6:21
For where your treasure is, there your heart will be also.

During a weekend shift at the small county hospital I sat in my candy striper uniform and held the frail hand of my critically ill grandmother. She told me of the near death experience that she had endured the night before. She described an experience involving long banquet tables laden with beautiful flowers and every type of fruit imaginable. She described lovely angels pouring water and wine from golden pitchers. She described the music that played continuously. Most importantly, she described Jesus sitting at the head of the table.
The staff of the hospital labeled my grandmother as "confused" and "delirious".
The message that she relayed to our family for the rest of her life was that nothing on this earth is equivalent to the richness of eternal life in heaven.

Heavenly father, we pray for the clarity and wisdom to focus on the important things, as this will ensure everlasting life. Amen

A tribute to my inspirational Grandmother,
Lee Norton Parks
By her Granddaughter Janice Brashear MSN, BC-PMHNP

Day 26

" 2 And after six days Jesus took with him Peter and James and John, and led them up a high mountain by themselves. And he was transfigured before them."

Every one of us loves to be on the mountaintop in life and to experience the blessings of the vistas. We yearn for easier times and struggle during the tough valleys of life. Yet it is in the struggle that we seek the Lord for strength. It is in the depths of despair that His promises are made real. Jesus is transfigured, and thus with us, every step of the journey. We do not need to seek future blessings, for we have already experienced the greatest joy, His grace, which is sufficient and saves us.

Because of Jesus
Laurie Anne Ferguson, DNP, APRN, FNP-C, FAANP
Dean and Associate Professor Loyola University New Orleans College of Nursing and Health

Day 27

Hi beautiful people!

My quick (and simple) bio includes that I'm a fairly new PNP. Graduated 3 years ago from Stonybrook University, and working in a school-based health clinic for the last 2 of them, after returning to graduate school in my late 40s, (what was I thinking!) Lol!

I'm married 28 yrs. to a wonderful (and very supportive) husband, have 3 children (oldest 2 in local colleges) and a 16 year old, help me Lord! But I love The Lord with all my heart and am grateful every day that HE's allowed me to understand that even in the simplest of tasks or encounters I may have with my patients, there's always an opportunity to share the love of Jesus in flesh. Nursing is not only our job, it's our calling.

Especially in this last decade, I've learned to really STOP and ENJOY the view/s, quality time, and shared spaces with my loved ones throughout it. Tomorrow is not promised, and struggles and troubles follow us daily (NOBODY is exempt from them). Psalm 34:19 reminds us that "The righteous person may have many troubles, but The Lord delivers him from them all." Today is here to conquer, and yesterday's precious moments give us hope and courage to press on towards victories still ahead. Life is a continuum of sweet spots and some equally bitter ones. In the meantime, I'll continue to share my smile in hopes to give hope, extend my hands to walk alongside, and apply my skills as a nurse/nurturer to enhance life even when that includes death; not only because HIS Word says in Luke 6:38 that giving of myself "will be returned back to me, pressed down, shaken together and running over" — but because I find pleasure in serving HIM whilst I serve others. HE's always taken care of me ... HE's never failed me yet ... HE'll never leave me nor forsake me. And that same promise is for YOU!

Prayer: Thank You Dear Father because "YOU have not given me a spirit of fear, but a spirit of power, love and of a sound mind." (2nd Timothy 1:7). So today I choose to Trust in YOU for EVERYTHING, with all of my heart, and I will not lean on my own understanding; and in all my ways I'm submitting to YOU, believing in YOUR promises, that YOU would make my paths straight." (Proverbs 3:5-6). Thank YOU in advance for finishing the work in me, Your child ...

Carmen Cruz Quintero, RN-C, MSN, PNP
New York City

Day 28

Shining Our Lights on Bright

One morning on my commute to work around 5 am, I was talking and praying to God starting out my drive. Praying for the day, praying to keep everyone safe, praying for safe travels, praying that safe care would be given at the hospital that day, praying to bring my lost family to church, everything that I normally pray about. About that time, I came upon a dense fog. You know as you drive through fog, you must turn down your lights to dim. After I turned them to dim, God spoke to me. He said as Christians, we are to shine our light of Jesus to everyone. But, our lights go dim sometimes. Like the fog overtaking everything in our line of sight on the road, worldly things will cloud our vision, diming our bright lights.

Many times in the Bible, it talks about God's shining light or for us to shine our lights in one form or another. When we shine our lights, we are not just being bright and bubbly. We are shining the light of Jesus to others. Matthew 5:14 tell us "You are the light of the world. A city set on a hill cannot be hidden"… and Matthew 5:16 says "let your light so shine before men, that they may see your good works, and glorify your Father which is in heaven." We are to let our lights shine bright before others to show them the Glory of God. God uses us as his disciples here on Earth. He wants us to shine brightly for others, so they can learn about Him and want to have an intimate relationship with him as well.

Dear Lord, I pray that I shine your light daily upon those who are lost that they may seek you. In Jesus Name, I Pray, Amen.

By Yalanda Scalf, MSN, RN
PMNHP Student at Frontier Nursing University
House Manager at Saint Joseph London
Adjunct Faculty at University of Cumberlands

Day 29

"Let us not become weary in doing good, for at the proper time we will reap a harvest if we do not give up."

Sometimes we find ourselves educating the same patient on the same health hazards over and over without anything getting through to them. Then, one day they surprise you by explaining how they lowered their A1c or how many days they've gone without a cigarette. This bible verse is a good reminder not to give up on the patient. You may be their only teammate.

John Watson APRN

"Therefore, as God's chosen people, holy and dearly loved, clothe yourselves with compassion, kindness, humility, gentleness and patience." Col 3:12 NIV

Most of us will admit, if we are truthful with ourselves and others that being compassionate and kind isn't always easy at the end of a long shift or in an atmosphere of ungodly people. After hours of working and meeting others needs compassion falls short when we are talked down to by a physician or co-worker or treated rudely by a patient's family. We quietly take whatever is handed to us most of the time, but inside we are just wanting to run away, cry, talk back, or respond in kind. Usually our faces show the despair or hurt we feel. Yet as Christians we are called to be "clothed" with compassion, humility, kindness, patience, and gentleness. This is a work that must be done inside our hearts in order for others to see these, "clothes" on the outside. So, what's the answer? In the midst of all that is happening, begin praying for them. You will both feel better once prayers have been lifted and your countenance will radiate the compassion and kindness of the Lord!

Lord, I ask that as I deal with people today, you would give me your eyes to see them as you see them. Grant me wisdom, love and compassion for every one you place in front of me today. In Jesus' name, Amen.

Robin Argyle, APRN, FNP-c
FNP in the urgent care setting, and Co-founder of Nurses with a Mission. It is my desire to go around the world and USA bringing hope to the hopeless and medical care to those who have little or none. MSN graduate of Frontier Nursing University Class 100. Hyden, Kentucky.

Robin Argyle, APRN, FNP-c, CNP

"For I know the plans I have for you", declares the Lord, "plans to prosper you and not to harm you plans to give you hope and a future. Then you will call on me and come and pray to me, and I will listen to you. You will seek me and find me when you seek me with all your heart".
Jeremiah 29:11-13

God has always had our best interest in mind. We sometime struggle to understand the whys and how's of this world because we cannot see the big picture. The God of the universe is the only one that knows everything about each one of His children. He knows which decision we will make in every situation. Romans 8:28 says, "And we know that in all things God works for the good of those who love Him, who have been called according to His purpose". He wants only good for his children, therefore we need to come to Him regularly through prayer asking for His guidance.

I love Jeremiah 12 - "Then you will call on me and come and pray to me, and I will listen to you". God is telling us in His word that He will listen to us when we pray. It is so awesome to have a loving Father that is always available to listen to our needs. A loving Father that answers in different ways in His timing, which is according to His plan for us. His answer may come through a closed door, a devotion that speaks directly to us or through another one of His children. The hard part is waiting on His timing. We are a nature of the times and we want an answer in our timing, which usually means now! Through my years, I have learned that His timing is always better than my timing and His way is always better than my way!

Jeremiah 29:13 reminds us that we have to seek Him with our whole heart if we want to find Him. God doesn't want His children to be lukewarm; He wants us to seek Him with our whole heart. I have found that I hear His plans for me much better when my heart is totally dedicated to Him. Jesus gave His all on the cross for our sins and we own Him our all for His gift of eternity.

May God give you the strength to wait on His timing and the peace to accept His plan for your life.

Teresa Rhew, APRN, FNP
I live in Bald Knob Arkansas. I am married to an amazing husband and my best friend Justin and have three amazing kiddos - Emily, Ryan and Jayden.

Day 32

Philippians 4:12 "I know what it is to be in need, and I know what it is to have plenty. I have learned the secret of being content in any and every situation, whether well fed or hungry, whether living in plenty or in want".

This is the message that the Apostle Paul wrote to the Philippians. This message was written from a dark and dirty prison cell. He had been arrested and accused of treason and was facing the possibility of execution. He had lost everything – including his freedom. One might deduct from the content of his writings that he was on "death row". This is the message of one whose heart was right with God.

Dear Father, we pray for the ability to trust in you, even when our circumstances are not of our choosing. We also pray for the wisdom to appreciate the many blessings that are sent down from heaven. It is in your name that we pray – Amen

Janice Brashear MSN, BC-PMHNP

Day 33

Psalm 91: 9 "For Jehovah is my refuge. I choose the God above all Gods to shelter me."
As the Bible says, man is created in God's image. We as humans, having the image and likeness of God, are gifted with the miracle of life from the womb. We are placed on this earth for a reason. Throughout varying stages of our lives, we search for that reason. We continue to search for that reason in this often chaotic and busy world we live in. We are faced with multiple distractions. We need to choose God above all the shelter us from the many storms of life. We are blessed with a direct connection to God through prayer. He knows our heart's desires even before we speak. God is our refuge and shelter; He protects us as parents protect their children. Additionally, Psalm *91:11-12 "For He orders His angels to protect you wherever you go, they will steady you with their hands to keep you from stumbling against the rocks on the trail."* Do you ever wonder how you were led to something or someone? Do you get moments when you asked how you were able to accomplish certain things against all the odds? Because as you chose God as your shelter, He sends His Angels to protect and guide you. I am a firm believer that we always need God's guidance and protection, no matter where we are. God guides us and speaks to us in many ways. We may not realize it at that time. God may show his angels in the form of a good friend, a mentor, a mother or father figure, someone who takes you under their wings. That is God's divine providence.

Dear God, thank you for the opportunity to praise you. Please forgive us for the times we were not able to heed your guidance or your call. We yearn to be showered with your graces. Please continue to guide us to be beacons in this world, spreading your light and love. While we do this, please continue to send your angels to protect us against the arrows that fly by night or day. We long to live by your glory and do your will. Amen.

Maria (Cristy) Murray
APRN, FNP-C

Day 34

1 Samuel 16:7: But the Lord said to Samuel, "Do not look at his appearance or at his physical stature, because I have refused him. For the Lord does not see as man sees; for man looks at the outward appearance, but he Lord looks at the heart."

I've always loved this scripture. As a woman, I can easily get distracted about my body, my clothes, and the outward "first impression" that I try to portray about who I am. But the truth is, *I am a child of God* first and foremost. When I allow myself to start caring more about my outward appearance (whether that be weight, wearing makeup, having nice clothes, or appearing confident), and less about my heart and spirit that is when Satan has room to sneak into my thoughts. It is during this time that Satan starts to whisper, "You aren't good enough. You aren't pretty enough. You aren't strong enough. They don't like you. You're fat." Add in whatever it is that Satan whispers to you.
Then, take the time to pray for God to show you who He created you to be. Sister, he created you for big things! He created you for a purpose! You were made in His image! I promise you that if you start meditating on these things and asking God to lead you as you navigate through your days, weeks, and years – God will reveal beautiful things about just how truly beautiful you are!

Heavenly Father, thank you for making us in your image. Help us to find the beauty within our souls and within the souls of others. Help us to stop focusing on our outward appearance and place our attention on our heart and spirit – which was beautifully made to mirror your love, compassion and caring spirit.

By Brittany Kurtz APRN, FNP-C
Nurse practitioner with Pediatric Pulmonology at the University of Louisville in Louisville, KY

Day 35

As a young girl I remember growing up listening to Kids' Praise Music and loving the stirring of my soul. To praise God brought me joy. But this feeling was not only happiness in singing, but based on Biblical truth! In Psalms 100, verses 1 through 5 we hear the call to:

¹ Shout for joy to the LORD, all the earth.
² Worship the LORD with gladness;
   come before him with joyful songs.
³ Know that the LORD is God.
   It is he who made us and we are his;
   we are his people, the sheep of his pasture.
⁴ Enter his gates with thanksgiving
   and his courts with praise;
   give thanks to him and praise his name.
⁵ For the LORD is good and his love endures forever;
   his faithfulness continues through all generations.

The mantra to make a joyful noise followed me through childhood beginning my walk as a Christian, through my young adulthood as I became a wife then mother, and all throughout my career. From nursing assistant to nurse practitioner, I carried the joy with me in my heart and served gladly, knowing I am an extension of his work, a daughter of God. There have been occasions that I was even blessed to share praise with patients and families, most notably during times of strife. As a hospice nurse, one of my dear patients was dying from end-stage chronic obstructive pulmonary disease. The only refuge he found was in worship music.

As a songwriter I felt compelled to create a song reflecting a journey from ignorance, strife and struggling into the welcoming arms of our Lord. The family tells me he was listening to it as he died, bringing comfort, not only to them, but to me. They even asked me to share that praise at his funeral. What an honor! Years later, a colleague asked me to sing Ave Maria and The Lord's Prayer over her dying patient and for the audience of his family; I was humbled, reluctant at first. But the spirit moved me to serve Him and bring blessings for their wounded spirits. In honoring God in that moment, I, too, received such a blessing. It was a privilege to provide such spiritual solace in trying times. I have been blessed to have several instances such as these over the years.

Yet, we must also find times of plenty and of happiness to pray through song, not merely sadness or pain. Music offers another avenue to communicate with and for God. So let us pray that our words, whether spoken or sung, intercede for ourselves or for others. I pray that your song reflects your joy and gladness, bringing you closer in your faith and walk with Christ. Make our words pleasing to your ears, Oh God; may we lift our voice to worship you; may our praise be a beacon to others, shining a light for others to come to you through their storms. Amen.

His Music in Me
By Michelle Leigh Arroyo, MSN, APRN, FNP-BC
Hospitalist Nurse Practitioner, NP student preceptor, and Doctoral student.

Peter reminds us that perspective is important. In 2 Peter 3:8-9 he writes "But do not forget this one thing, dear friends: With the Lord a day is like a thousand years, and a thousand years are like a day. The Lord is not slow in keeping his promise, as some understand slowness. He is patient with you, not wanting anyone to perish, but everyone to come to repentance".

Sometimes it is difficult to wait on God's perfect timing. It is important to remember that he is not indifferent to our struggles while we are here on Earth. His perspective of time is not like ours. He created time; therefore is above it. As the creator of our rules of science, He is not bound by those laws. Time in Heaven is eternity, so an era in time appears as a moment in history. Since God's perspective of time is unlike ours in that He is capable of rising above it. He waits patiently while we are in turmoil. He waits for us to recognize that He alone is sovereign, and He is a bigger than our problems. His unending patience with us is to allow us ample time to recognize our need for Him for salvation, and to allow us time to seek Him, learn about Him, and to develop a relationship with Him.

Dear God, I pray that all who read these words and their families know you as their personal savior. Let these pages be a legacy that ripples through relationships and through time so that all may know you. Please continue to lead, guide, direct, and protect as we continue to seek you and give you glory. Amen.

By: Sherri McGauley, MSN, CRNFA, NP-C. Lifelong career in surgery, specializing in orthopedics, with an emphasis on spine and upper extremity.

Day 37

Be strong and very courageous (Joshua 1:7)

Nursing is not for the faint of heart. You are one day protecting the life of a helpless neonate or the safety of the aged dementia patient. You are the final protection for a helpless homeless individual who has entered the healthcare system not of his/her own volition confused and angry. You are the keeper of safety for the victim of violence. You are allowed to enter the very private environment of the living and the dying and allow your own family to suffer while you minister to others. Nursing is a calling, a ministry that only God can prepare you for and leaning not on your own understanding but looking through the eyes of a loving Savior will impact others in ways you will never know.
Prayer – Father God, help us to reach through the difficult times, the times where we want to say, what about me, and see those in need through your eyes. May we have the grace to give more, the wisdom of what to say, the kindness to extend to the unlovable, the compassion that is needed at just the right moment and always, yes always, love others as you have loved us.

Julie Eddins AG-ACNP-BC Orthopedic Oncology Nurse Practitioner Barnes Jewish Hospital, St Louis, MO privileged to care for people in need of hope.

Day 38

"Blessed be the Lord God of Israel for ever and ever. And all the people said, Amen, and praised the Lord." –I Chronicles 16:36

Every Sunday morning at our church, we sing the Doxology in English. At my husband's home church in Hawaii though, the Doxology is sung in Hawaiian. When I try to sing the words in Hawaiian, I stumble over the many vowel sounds, but I always get the last word right. It is "Amene"—amen with an "e". Every Sunday morning in MS, my husband and I quietly add the "e" to the Amen at the end of the song and breathe a prayer for our family and friends in Hawai'i.

Thank You, Lord, that each of us can praise You in any language with the simplest or the grandest of words. You understand us—just the way we are. –"Amene."

In loving memory of my father, a Methodist minister, Rev. M. Rowley
Ruth Chong, MSN, FNP-C
Jackson, MS

John 14:1
"Do not let your hearts be troubled. You believe in God; believe also in me."
As a little girl, my Grandmother, Estelle Ethele Campbell, was a strong woman of faith. When things became difficult for me in life, she would always say "Keep your mind on Jesus." I did not realize it then, but time spent with her was for a greater good.
My Grandmother lived in such a way that, she expected to see her 14 to also see heaven. There will always be one contrary person in the group. However, the prayers of the righteous "will prevail." When my Grandmother's oldest son was placed in Hospice, God allowed me to speak and hear his confession of faith, to give my family the peace they needed.
We may never know the extent of the preparation for God's work. However, if you have prayed the prayer of faith "Trust God." Because when we trust God, he will surely give us the peace, regardless of the crisis.

LaTangra M. McIntosh, MSN, ARNP-BC, LMHC

Day 40

"He gives strength to the weary and increases the power of the weak (Isaiah 40:29)

So many times throughout my career as a nurse, I have faced genuine burnout. At the precise moment I feel like quitting, God speaks to me through my patients. Last week, I went to a dialysis clinic I haven't been to in months, and as soon as a patient saw me she began to weep saying, "I have missed you so much. I thought I was never going to see you again". It's those small moments that help me remember how much I still have yet to give.

Father, use me as your vessel. May my patients not see me but You through me. Don't allow my hands, my mind, and my heart to falter as I continue your work.

Christina Hartshorn, BSN, FNP student, hemodialysis nurse.

Day 41

I once heard a story that stuck with me. It was about three masons who were going about their jobs building a church. Each was doing his job but the real story was how each man viewed his job. When asked, "What are you doing?" the first man said, "I'm doing my job to collect a pay check". The second man replied, "I'm laying brick, building this wall". The third man responded, "I'm building a beautiful Cathedral where people will come to give praise to God for their many blessings." Andrian Rogers once said that "Wisdom is looking at life from God's point of view". How can we know God's point of view and how do we get His perspective so that in our lives we build Cathedrals instead of merely collecting the paycheck. Isaiah 55:8-9 says, "For my thoughts are not your thoughts, neither are your ways my ways," declares the Lord. "As the heavens are higher than the earth, so are my ways higher than your ways and my thoughts than your thoughts." Learning about God is a life long endeavor, but as we go about our daily lives, we should strive for wisdom so that we may see the world from God's perspective. Our trials today give us perspective to solve problems in the future and help others to do the same, perhaps leading them to Christ.

Dear Heavenly Father, I pray today for our country and for those reading this today that you give them correct perspective in what You have allowed into our lives. May we continue to seek You. Amen

Sherri McGauley, MSN, CRNFA, NP-C. Lifelong career in surgery, specializing in orthopedics, with an emphasis on spine and upper extremity.

We all experience deep soul weariness in different ways and for different reasons. Our lives are complex. We see emotional heartbreaks and the consequences of sin. It surpasses our understanding. Simple platitudes "Cheer up!" "Things will get better." They do nothing for us because our burdens are not simple. God is strong enough to relieve our heaviness and weariness.

Bible Passage: Come to me, all you who are weary and burdened, and I will give you rest. Take my yoke upon you and learn from me, for I am gentle and humble in heart, and you will find rest for your souls. For my yoke is easy and my burden is light (Matthew 11:28-30).

Prayer: O God, I come to you at the beginning of this day confessing my weakness and claiming your strength. Lead me by the hand through all the paths of this day, I pray. Amen.
Bio:
In loving memory of the life and ministry of Marlena Sharrett.
By Dr. Melissa Townsend, DNP, ARNP, FNP-BC
Pain Management Nurse Practitioner at Vigilant Health Systems

Day 43

Proverbs 17: 22 states, "A cheerful heart is good medicine, but a crushed spirit dries up the bones." Often times when our patients come into our office, they are filled with anxiety, depression, and fear. The last thing they need is to come in to seek assistance from a healthcare professional and they enter the room in a precipitous manner, possess a flat affect, collect information devoid of any eye contact, and appear to be more interested in the electronic medical record than the patient, himself. When we treat our patients in this manner, the patient leaves feeling worse than when they arrived. Greeting a patient with a huge smile, making eye contact while collecting pertinent information, and exemplifying a spirit of compassion can make patients feel better because they get a perception that someone actually cares. Jehovah Rapha, my prayer is for you to fill our hearts with joy and love for what we possess in our hearts is spoken from our mouths. Let our words be those of compassion, encouragement, and love to inspire the lives of our patients and to give honor to you.

Khoshunda Monique Williams MSN, APRN, FNP-C University of Texas at Tyler Family Nurse Practitioner at Wellness Pointe in Kilgore, Texas

Day 44

"For I know the plans I have for you, " declares the LORD, "plans to prosper you and not to harm you, plans to give you hope and a future." (Jeremiah 29.11)

When we become Christians, our life is not guaranteed to be perfect. We will still have pain, uncertainty, struggles and bad times. God shows me time and time again, through depression, sadness, abuse (mental and physical) and codependency that He loves and cares for His children. Since the beginning of my relationship with Christ at the age of 26, though I struggle, I have never been hopeless or alone. I may fall and fail but my faith is never faltering and I am thankful we can believe His promise that He has wonderful plans for us.

O God, I pray that the person that is reading this verse feels your love and hope right this moment. Please show them they are never alone and can always believe you know the beginning, middle and end to their story and that it is MAGNIFICENT. Amen.

Christine Hunt, FNP-C, APRN
Kansas City Medicine Partners – blessed to take care of the geriatrics

Day 45

A Letter to the Romans from Paul, a servant of Jesus Christ, called to be an Apostle

"For I am persuaded, that neither death, nor life, nor angels, nor principalities, nor powers, nor things present, nor things to come, nor height, nor depth, nor any other creature, shall be able to separate us from the love of God, which is in Christ Jesus our Lord." (Romans 8: 38-39)

By this scripture, I am reminded that God's love never wavers for us. We are forever his children and loved beyond comprehension. Whenever you feel abandoned by family, friends or co-workers, stop and allow peace to enter your heart through prayer. Through peace, you will understand God's love is always there for you, as man will disappoint, but God is always there, waiting for us to turn to him for help and guidance. Prayer helps us quiet the voices that cause us to doubt ourselves, and reminds us that God loves us and is guiding us along the way. Be aware of God's love in your life, he is always there.

In prayer I give thanks and love to Jesus Christ who died for our sins and who demonstrated true and unwavering love for all people. I give thanks and love to God, the Father, for His unconditional love for all of us, His children. Amen.

My eternal love and gratitude is in memory of Ruby G. Edmonds, my Mother, who suffered from early childhood physical and mental wounds until her death at age 74. I will love you forever Mom. Witnessing your suffering, made me into the compassionate and caring Nurse Practitioner I am today. You never doubted God nor His Son, Jesus Christ; for in His love, you found your strength. By Emma S. (Edmonds, Ampezzan) Bowser, MSN, RN, ANP-BC

Day 46

God, Create a new, clean heart within me. Fill me with pure thoughts and holy desires, ready to please you. (Psalms 51:10 TPT)

How refreshing at any time of the day we can go to the Lord and pray this prayer and meditate upon it. If something is bothering us, we may need to check our motives and reset our heart and thoughts. The word instructs us to guard our hearts and minds through Christ Jesus, and this verse is powerful to address both our hearts and thoughts. How wonderful are the instructions of the Lord, he is waiting to renew a right spirit within us, His beautiful beloved children.

Prayer: Precious Heavenly Father, thank you for this day and another chance to serve You. Father we pray to surrender our hearts to You, that you may create a new, clean heart and steadfast spirit that we may be able to walk in holy desires ready to please you. Burn off the dross and cares of the world and encourage us this day through the power of the Holy Spirit, In Christ name we pray, amen.

Amen.

In loving memory of the life and service of my brother who served in the United States Armed Forces Leon Harkinson
By Stephanie Hull, BSN, RN-BC, Graduate Nursing Student at University of Southern Indiana, Evansville, Indiana

Day 47

Nooks and Crannies

Psalms 42:7 "deep calls to deep" is a portion of scripture that speaks of God reaching deep into the spirit of His children. Through intimate time with the Father we know Him more deeply.

The Holy Spirit desires to search the depths of our hearts, minds and souls. Allow Him to do so. He will perform a DEEP CLEANING. He wants you look at the crevices where the little crumbs, tiny debris, and minute dust particles hide. He desires to deal with the little stuff in our hearts. He will look deep if we allow Him.

After we accept Christ, the Holy Spirit soon begins to deal with us regarding our sin. Then as we have walked with HIM for a time, the surface is clean and the most visible sins seem to be conquered. But God is speaking, "I want the tiny dirty stuff" ......a word, a thought, an attitude, or the undisciplined area. When we get intimate with the Father, He will reveal those things hidden in the nooks and crannies.

I needed to clean my kitchen and I needed to pray. My house was quit, so I began to do both. My mind began to be totally focused on God, yet I continued to clean. I asked God to speak to me in the everyday and the mundane. He quickly answered. "I do.... you don't listen. It's all about your focus and attention. I want to do a DEEP CLEAN." Remember I am cleaning my kitchen. He prompts me to look inside the cabinet doors, the kick plate beneath the lower cabinets, the edge where the tile meets the trim mold, the oven door creases, and the refrigerator when everything is take out. There was a lot of dirt that has previously gone unnoticed. A lot of things get revealed when we allow the Holy Spirit to go into the deep places.

Look at how you love others and reflect on each relationship. Cultivate each one and He will show you how to love DEEPLY. Ask the Father to reveal wrong thoughts and attitudes. Let Him show you any crumb of impurity in the deep nooks and crannies. Listen to the Holy Spirit prompting you to correct those little areas in your life that are unlike the Father. As we allow Him to do the work of DEEP CLEANING, we are made more like Him.

In loving memory of my father Rev. Jerry Crouse. By Sherry Whitby MSN, APRN, FNP-C. Christian Family Medicine Trenton

Day 48

In all your ways submit to Him and he will make your paths straight.
Proverbs 3:6

The "List"

Are you so busy you need a "to do" list? I know I do. On my list I have several priority items and many "necessary" items, such as sending out bills, cleaning the cupboard, mailing a birthday present or scrubbing the floor. Is spending time with God on your list? Many times our lists are so long we forget what is really important. Many times we don't stop to think about what God wants us to do. What if God wrote your "To-Do" list one day? What (or who) do you think would be on that list? Look at your "to-Do" list today and make sure God is present on that list and that you are doing what He wants you to do. Maybe you need to forgive someone, face your fears, post something inspirational on social media, pray for a friend (or enemy) or volunteer in your community. We're all busy, but are we too busy for God's work?
Prayer: Heavenly Father, help me to listen to your plan for me. Help me to look for ways to serve you every single day. Let your love shine through me. Amen.

By Dr. Julie Benton Parve DNP, FNP-BC, APNP
Associate Professor- Concordia University Wisconsin
Graduate Nursing
Medical Director- Hope Without Borders

Day 49

John 15:12   *This is my commandment, that you love one another as I have loved you.*

As nurse practitioners we are called to care for people from all walks of life. Sometimes, they reach in and grab our hearts-these clients are a joy to care for. However, there are also clients who are challenging to provide care to for a variety of reasons. Attitudes, life choices, unrealistic family members, or any number of things can challenge us. In these cases, this commandment rings true and we should remember Jesus died for them too. He loves us all equally even on our worst day. If we honor this commandment it can make a difference in the care of our clients and perhaps even their outcomes.

Lord, help us to be true followers who love others as you love us, even when loving them seems difficult or counter intuitive to our belief system. Your sacrifice is a gift to all who will receive it. Help us to be ever mindful of this gift as we care for others. Amen

By Dr. Elizabeth M. Long DNP, APRN, GNP-BC, CNS, Assistant Professor Lamar University Dishman School of Nursing, Beaumont, Texas

Day 50

"Look at the birds of the air, for they neither sow nor reap nor gather into barns; yet your heavenly Father feeds them. Are you not of more value than they?" (Matthew 6:26)

God's love was revealed to me through the story of my fur baby, "Kitty." She was an orange tabby stray cat that showed up at my doorstep a few weeks before Christmas 2013. She was so skinny and it was apparent she was starving. My husband said, "If you feed her, she will never leave." Despite this fact, I could not ignore her desperate meows and sweet nature as she brushed up against my leg and purred as I opened my front door. I just could not leave her in that condition. I gave her food and she became part of the family.

Fast-forward to year 2014 and I had this great idea to get a family photo with her and my two dogs. The photographer was located over 2 hours from where we lived so we loaded up the SUV with our fur babies and headed to our appointment. Midway through the trip, we decide to stop at Michaux State Forest so the dogs could stretch. While I was getting the dogs back in the vehicle, my husband decided he would place a leash on Kitty and let her out for a stretch. She immediately darted off into the woods with leash dragging behind her and my husband hit the grass face first as he lunged to stop her in his attempt to grab the leash. She was gone. I was mortified.

I promptly posted an unspoken prayer request on my Facebook page. We then called her name and thoroughly searched for her. My husband hiked into the woods and I drove around the area seeking her. Eight hours later, we were still seriously searching and it had reached an urgent level, as it was getting dark. I remember feeling panic at the thought of never finding her. I just could not leave her in that lost condition. She was so valued and loved!

At this point, I remembered we had her treat bag with us. I suggested my husband go into the woods one more time and take the bag with him and shake it to lure her to him. Meanwhile, I stayed in the car with the dogs and pleaded with God to help us. The Lord gently reminded me of how much He loves me. He desperately searches for me when I lose my way and He is so heartbroken when I stray from Him. Despite all my failures and flaws, I am so valuable that He leaves the other sheep to search for me. He loved me so much that He sent His Son for me. There is no greater love.

The realization was overwhelming when I compared my feelings of love and desperation over my lost Kitty and how God must feel about us when we go astray. It was very apparent to me that my little prayer and request to find Kitty was so minor in comparison to what other people may have been praying for that day but I was also acutely aware that God sees and cares for the smallest details in our lives, even my Kitty. It was at this point the Lord told me He heard my prayers and I knew everything would be okay. As I lifted my head up and opened my eyes, I immediately saw my husband walking out of the woods with Kitty in his arms!

Dear Lord,
Help me to realize the extent of your love and the sacrifice you made for me. Forgive me if I have strayed from you. Renew me today and help me to show your love and concern to everyone I meet. I pray that my patients will come to know you and experience your healing touch. Thank you for your concern about the smallest details in life and thank you for not leaving me in my lost condition. I love you, Lord. Amen.

In loving memory of the life of Roseanna Landis and Robert Hooe, Sr.
Dedicated to the memory of my fur baby, Cinnamon
By: Angela Hooe, MSN, FNP-C
Attended Simmons College and Shenandoah University
Avid animal lover and mom to Tina and Kitty

Day 51

To all those hurt souls, may you find the peace you so desperately need and crave by trusting in Him.

Prayer:
Dear Mister Jesus,
Shine upon us your heavenly glow.
Within my heart and soul doth Lord Jesus grow.
Our Lord and Savior is one to be praised,
By giving thanks each and every day.
Not doubting Him we shall all rise,
To the Kingdom of Heaven way up high.
Once again I Thank You Lord for all that you have done.
Without you, I fear the battle has just begun.
In Jesus name, Amen

Scripture tells us that the battle is not between flesh and blood but rather it is against the rulers, authorities, the power of this dark world and against spiritual forces (Ephesians 6:13, NIV). We are to take comfort in the knowledge that God has a remedy for those of us who seek peace in the midst of chaos, and pain. He tells us to be anxious for nothing but in every situation, by prayer and petition, with thanksgiving, present your requests to God. And the peace of God, which transcends all understanding, will guard your hearts and your minds in Christ Jesus (Philippians 4:6-7, NIV). For Christians the battle has already been won, all we have to do is claim the victory (John 1 4:4, NIV).

Kristy Flores MSN, RN, FNP Student Walden University

Day 52

And He said to me, "My grace is sufficient for you, for My strength is made perfect in weakness." Therefore most gladly I will rather boast in my infirmities, that the power of Christ may rest upon me. (2 Corinthians 12:9)

Through our toughest times, He loves us and will not see us fall. His strength steps in where we fall short and become weak. He is the gap filler and our strength. We have to pray for Him to rain His power down on us.

Father, we pray that your strength and grace. Be our strength like no other. Fill us with Your strength where we are weak Lord! We praise your Holy Name, for we know it is You and not us that we do the things we once were too weak to do. We honor you and thank You. Amen.

Dedicated to my husband Corey, and 3 children, Jaden, Alex, and Nyla
By Anjeleigh Lonnette Robinson Partridge
Family Nurse Practitioner/Clinical Researcher
UNC Chapel Hill School of Medicine- Infectious Disease

Day 53

Paul wrote "I am convinced *and* confident of this very thing that He who has begun a good work in you will continue to perfect *and* complete it until the day of Christ Jesus the time of His return." (Philippians 1:6)

As believers we have to have full assurance in the promises of God that all of the works that He promised, He is faithful to perform. Like watching a seed grow from the ground and fruit to spring forth, we have to remain assured and steadfast in His promises, because His word will not return to us void.

Heavenly Father, strength our faith and remove any doubt that is in our hearts or minds in Your ability to complete what You promised. We know your ways are not ours, so Lord, as you shape us into Your will, we will continue to praise and magnify your glorious name. Amen.

Dedicated to my Mother, Yvonne S. Hailey
By Anjeleigh Lonnette Robinson Partridge
Family Nurse Practitioner/Clinical Researcher
UNC Chapel Hill School of Medicine- Infectious Disease

Day 54

Psalm 23:13, David says, "I would have despaired had I not believed that I would see the goodness of the LORD In the land of the living." As believers we must have faith and not faint.
We cannot fear and have faith. Faith allows us to sustain through the toughest of times. The posture of our hearts must be courageous, faithful, grateful and thankful.
Lord, we pray that you while we wait for the answer to our prays that we remain strong in You. We pray God that our faith is unshaken in Your promises to us. Lord, you may not answer in our time, but we know that Your time is better for us and is in Your will for our life. Amen.

By Anjeleigh Lonnette Robinson Partridge
Family Nurse Practitioner/Clinical Researcher
UNC School of Medicine- Infectious Disease

Day 54

I was late on an assignment during a time that I also was on a trip to the beach with my sister. I was trying my hardest to accomplish the assignment but would always come to road block. I told my sister, "I think I'm going to have to quit. This is beyond my capabilities." My sister replied, "Maybe it is, but it's not too complicated for God." She said we would pray about it and she would take the kids out so that I could work on it.

In the hustle, we forgot to pray. As I sat at the computer, feeling sorry for myself for missing yet another fun activity due to extra work, I tried hard to accomplish it, but could not. I cried and remembered that we never prayed together about it. I felt hopeless. A few seconds later there was a knock on the door and my niece was there because my sister had forgot her license. My niece stated as she left "Good luck on your paper. You'll do great. We just had prayer for you downstairs." Six people had joined in prayer for me!!

I sat down at the computer and every road block that had been thrown my way for weeks, was instantly torn down. I was amazed. I am grateful for God's wisdom and generosity. I ended up with an "A" on something that was out of my capability. If you are lacking wisdom, ASK! You will receive.

James 1:5 King James Version (KJV)

If any of you lack wisdom, let him ask of God, that giveth to all men liberally, and upbraideth not; and it shall be given him.

Dear Heavenly Father, please meet my sisters and brothers in Christ, where You met me that day and grant them the gift of wisdom and the knowledge that You are whom to seek for wisdom. Amen.

In honor of the faithfulness of my sister, Erica Butts. By Diana Niland, PhD candidate, APRN, FNP-C at WVU Medicine Potomac Valley Hospital/Potomac State College.

Day 55

"For I know the plans I have for you", declares the Lord, "plans to prosper you and not to harm you, plans to give you hope and a future". Jeremiah 29:11-12

So many times in life, our circumstance dictates our ability to truly have hope for something more optimal…a better grade…more profitable job…meaningful life ventures. We are so often unable to visualize and conceptualize the fact that God planned our life's journey before we were formed in our mother's womb. God knows what He has for us…but often our own shortsighted and impatient plans get in the way of His. I imagine He spends quite a lot of his day straightening up the messes we have found ourselves in. This verse in Jeremiah is an anchor of hope and a reminder of His constant vigilant watch over us. He has always gone before us, preparing a pathway of relevance, prosperity, connection and favor.

Dear God, Please remind us of your plans. When we have strayed from your path of purpose, please gently lead us back. Get our attention if you must. Grant us the connection of a church body that will lift us and encourage us. Thank you, dear God, for your nurses. Strengthen, enable and inspire them in your Holy work. Bless the hands and feet that serve you in this holy profession. In Jesus name, Amen

In loving memory of my granddaughter, Kaylie Jackson, your light is shining brightest in heaven. Janie Owens, FNP, DNP, Founder of Nurse Practitioner Community of Faith, Inc., Lexington, Kentucky.

Day 56

Put on the full armor of God so that you can take your stand against the devil's schemes. (Ephesians 6:11)

As Christians, we will face obstacles. The devil will attack us and bring temptations and enemies into our lives. This suffering can bring us depression, anxiety, and doubt. If we are not armed with scripture, faith, and a relationship with God, it becomes difficult to resist the temptations.

We need to be prepared to suffer, but we are also comforted that Jesus died on the cross and suffered for us, so that we are promised these trials are temporary. Thank you, God, for sacrificing your son, so that we have hope in You and in our eternal life.

Dear God,
   You know the battles I am facing and how my heart feels heavy at times. Clothe me with your strength and empower me to love my enemies and pray for them. Provide me with the armor to face each day and be a great example of your unconditional love. Let these trials strengthen mu faith so that I may witness to others.

By Tiffany Pottkotter, Psychiatric Nurse Practitioner, Promedica Physicians Behavioral Health

Day 57

"If you are given much, much will be required of you. If much is entrusted to you, much will be expected of you." (Luke 12:48)

In undergrad, one of my colleagues asked "Can you try not to do so much for your PowerPoints? It makes us look like we aren't doing anything." At the time, I could not understand why she felt that I should decrease especially when I was one of the lowest performers in our cohort.

Have you considered dimming your light to make others comfortable? Did you know that every time we as Christians say "yes" to others' expectations we are saying "no" to God's purpose for our lives? What I know for sure is that public speaking is my genius, a God-given gift or talent that comes naturally. But who would of thought that I would discover this in nursing school? Now I recognize that it was all part of his plan for me to one day marry my genius to my nursing skills to create a platform for others. Always remember, great gifts come with great responsibilities. Today, I challenge you to recognize your genius, put it to use, and shine on.

Father, I thank you for the gifts you have given me. I ask that you make it clear what you have anointed my hands to do. Today, I say "yes" to your will for my life and "no" to my fears of what man will do. Amen.

By Patrice Faye Little, DNP, FNP-BC

Founder of *NP Student Magazine* and Nurses in Media

Author of *Out of Crazy Born Genius: Reclaim Life After Abuse*

Clinical Instructor, Georgia State University – Perimeter College

Day 58

1 Peter 5:7
Cast all your cares upon him for he cares for you.

This truly represents how much God loves us and wants to be our provider. He does not say cast some of our cares but ALL of our cares upon him. God is our father and wants to absolutely be our source to supply all of our needs. When troubles arise, enter his courts with thanksgiving and praise. God is waiting and anticipating to hear our voice through prayer and worship. We let go and let God!

Dear Heavenly Father,

We bless your holy name. Holy, holy, holy, Lord God Almighty! Father we thank you for this moment to praise your name! Wonderful counselor! Mighty God! We adore you and bow down before you. Father you said according to 1 Peter 5:7 to cast all of our cares upon you because you care for us. We thank you for this blessing and operate in obedience giving you all of our cares in this moment (say them). Father your will be done.

In the name of Jesus the Christ,

Amen

Damali M. Marshall APRN, MSN, FNP-C
Founder of the Strategic Nurse Network
Family Nurse Practitioner | Dynamic Healthcare and Associates

Day 59

You will seek me and find me when you seek me with all your heart. (Jeremiah 29:13 NIV)

God absolutely loves when we seek his presence with our heart and mind. Our seeking him turns into worship and our worship includes ministering to God. Glory be to God! We worship and adore you GOD!! God speaks to us when there are still quiet moments in worship. Listen, he is speaking to you now! Surely his presences is here because God is omnipotent, omniscience and omnipresent. Oh how joyful we become when we realize GOD is a sound.

 Prayer:
Heavenly Father thank you for your goodness, mercy and favor. All praises be unto the King of King and Lord of Lords. O God, speak to us in this moment so we may know your voice. Father God, the word says my sheep listen to my voice; I know them and they follow me. (John 10:27 NIV) God speak to us today during the still quiet moments of worship.

In the name of Jesus Christ,

Amen

Damali M. Marshall APRN, MSN, FNP-C
Founder of the Strategic Nurse Network,
Family Nurse Practitioner | Dynamic Healthcare and Associates

"For God is not unjust. He will not forget how hard you have worked for him and how you have shown your love to him by caring for other believers, as you still do." Hebrews 6:10

When I finally realized my nursing career had been my calling and not just a career, I developed a new passion for caring for others that was deeper than I'd ever felt. As I follow God on new paths in my career, the enemy knows how to attack to try to sway me from God's plan. One way he does this is to make me feel unappreciated, used, and burnt out. He says I'm doing all this hard work for nothing; there are no compliments or praises for it. When these thoughts come creeping in and making me weary, God reminds me that my work is not in vain. He reminds me that my reward is in Him and he is just. The enemy thinks he's pulling me down, when, in fact, he is just reminding me to stay humble, to deny myself (again…) and turn my focus on God and the people He has placed in my path for me to serve.

Father, Thank you for leading me to a role where I can share your love and be your light. Help me to remember that you chose me for this purpose and that you never forget my efforts to serve you. Give me a heart of humility, as well as gratitude for the blessings you've already given me. Continue to be my strength and my joy in this world. Amen.

By Kayla Bauman, MSN, FNP-C
Family Practice Nurse Practitioner, Parkview Physicians Group
Student Nurse Midwife Frontier Nursing University

Romans 1:16 KJV For I am not ashamed of the gospel of Christ: for it is the power of God unto salvation to everyone that believeth; to the Jew first, and also the Greek.

There was a time very early on in my walk with Christ that I was afraid to share the goodness of the Lord. I was worried about what people would think, how they would look at me, or just the idea of rejection all together. As I grew stronger in my faith and saw all the wonderful things that God had done in my life and the lives of those around me, it became evident that those testimonies were to be shared to help others who needed hope, to know they were loved, and what God had done for me, He most certainly would and could do for them too.

I learned to listen to the Holy Spirit (that small still voice) and when prompted by the Holy Spirit to move, I pray, share, and speak the Word of God into others lives. It's amazing how a small pray can make a big change in someone's life! I now share with anyone who is has a heart and ears to receive God's Word and I know my Father is well pleased. I thank God for helping my get to this point in my life and being a blessing to the people He has placed in my path.

Prayer: Father, I thank You for teaching me in Your Word through your Son, Jesus, how important it is to share the Good News. I pray for all who love You to have the boldness of a Lion to share with each person they encounter. I pray that Your Word penetrates the hearts of those who are hurting, sickly, or just need to know they are "So Loved" by an awesome God, in Jesus Name I pray, Amen!

Julia Echols, MSN-FNP-BC

Follower of Christ

Si Dios quiere: If God wishes
Base on a sermon at First Church Boston
Delivered by Dr. Margaret A. Fitzgerald
DNP, FNP-BC, NP-C, FAANP, CSP, FAAN, DCC, FNAP
President, Fitzgerald Health Education Associates, Inc.
Family NP, Greater Lawrence (MA) Family Health Center
www.fhea.com peg@fhea.com

I am a family nurse practitioner, at the Greater Lawrence Family Health Center in Lawrence, MA, also known as the Immigrant City, at one of the nation's largest community health centers where we provide primary health care, from obstetrical to pediatrics to adult and elder health care in low income Latino community. Most but certainly not all of my patients and co-workers are deeply religious people, Catholic, Evangelical Christian, and Jehovah's Witness. I hear this term daily, Si Dios quiere, if God wishes. I dare say multiple times an hour. For that matter, after more than two decades serving this community, I find myself, a person of science, a Unitarian Universalist, saying it. I questions I ask myself often is why.

I can see a patient with pneumonia, pretty sick but doing well enough to be treated as an outpatient. I order the needed tests, carefully consider the clinical factors, prescribe an antibiotic, give advice on drinking fluids, what to watch for, when to come back for follow up, and let the person know that he will likely be feeling in a few days. Seems standard issue, systematic application of the scientific evidence. However, the visit is not yet complete. Either I or the patient, or perhaps both of us, will invariably add, a "Si Dio quiere", in other words, the recovery I, a person of science and reason, anticipate will occur shortly, will occur, if God wishes. What this means to me is- there is a force, that will help me focus to consider all the clinical factors in the face of an extraordinary busy day at clinic, that will bring me and the patient together into this relationship, for this brief period, there is a spirit that helps this person to heal. We will both call this strength up in our own way. My concept of a relationship with God, the Divine, is intensely personal and perhaps different than many of my patients, but I will be there, to share, and sometimes be the strength, the person needs to heal.

The intersection of science, healthcare and faith. I cannot pry these apart. Si Dios quiere is, in essence, a short prayer, an act to call attention to the pressing problem. Prayer, the dialogue between the person and the Divine.

I see people of all ages, pregnant women, babies, and kids, younger and older adults. I am privileged to serve these people, work with them to achieve the best help possible against some pressing odds.

I have told you how I make peace with incorporating faith into my practice. Do I believe this is reciprocated by my patients? The answer comes in shared moments.

- A mom smiles and places her 7 day-old baby in my arms. We hug and admire this beautiful miracle. Gloria a Dios (Glory to God).

- I see a middle aged man who is recovering from a stroke. We embrace, giving thanks for the restoration of health. Garcia a Dios (Thanks to God).

- I see an older woman with failing kidneys who prays for me nightly. El Señor es contigo. The Lord is with you.

I hope I help carry some of their burdens in sickness, suffering and death as I also share in their joy.

A prayer from my faith tradition I offer.

Open my eyes, that I might see Your face in everyone I encounter this day, myself included.

Open my ears that I might hear Your voice in whatever forms it takes.

Open my hands, which I might freely give whatever is mine to share.

Open my heart that I might live and love more fully in You.

Great blessings to us all, si Dios quiere.

Made in the USA
Columbia, SC
17 August 2023

21764438R00043